The Wee book of Irish Blessings, Toasts and Proverbs.

By
John William Tuohy

Irish Blessings, Toasts and Proverbs

* * * * *

For Mary

*

Irish Proverbs: Drinking

A man takes a drink, the drink takes a drink, the drink takes the man.

It's the first drop that destroys you, there's no harm at all in the last.

If it's drowning you're after, don't torment yourself with shallow water.

Irish Proverbs: Work & Idleness

It's not a delay to stop and sharpen the scythe.

It's a dirty bird that won't keep its own nest clean.

Keep your shop and your shop will keep you.

A bad workman quarrels with his tools.

Unwillingness easily finds an excuse.

Lose an hour in the morning and you'll be looking for it all day.

Laziness is a heavy burden.

Poverty waits at the gates of idleness.

Irish Proverbs: Youth & Old Age

Praise the ripe field not the green corn.

Young people don't know what old age is, and old people forget what youth was.

The schoolhouse bell sounds bitter
in youth and sweet in old age.

The older the fiddle the sweeter
the tune.

As the old cock crows, the young
cock learns.

The old dog for the hard road and
leave the pup on the path.

Irish Proverbs: Romance & Marriage

It's easy to halve the potato where there's love.

If you want praise, die. If you want blame, marry.

Beauty won't make the kettle boil.

Honey is sweet, but don't lick it off a briar.

Don't show your skin to a person who won't cover it.

A man cannot grow rich without his wife's leave.

Irish Proverbs: Character & Honor

Better good manners than good looks.

It is more difficult to maintain honour than to become prosperous.

Promise is in honor's debt.

Forgetting a debt doesn't mean it's paid.

A man may live after losing his life but not after losing his honor.

Better to be a man of character than a man of means.

Better the trouble that follows death than the trouble that follows shame.

If you come up in this world be sure not to go down in the next.

Who gossips with you will gossip of you.

Lie down with dogs and you'll rise with fleas.

Irish Proverbs:
Opportunity

You'll never plough a field by turning it over in your mind.

You won't learn to swim on the kitchen floor.

Slow is every foot on an unknown path.

There are fish in the sea better than have ever been caught.

A combed head sells the feet.

Don't make little of your dish for it may be an ignorant fellow who judges it.

If your messenger is slow, go to meet him.

Many a sudden change takes place on an unlikely day.

Irish Proverbs: Fortune & Wealth

Enough and no waste is as good as a feast.

Cut your coat according to your cloth.

He who has water and peat on his own farm has the world his own way.

A cat can look at a king.

It is not the same to go to the king's house as to come from it.

The life of an old hat is to cock it.

There never came a gatherer but a scatterer came after him.

Better be sparing at first than at last.

If you buy what you don't need you might have to sell what you do.

Hunger is a good sauce.

A heavy purse makes a light heart.

Heaven's leac na teine (stone before the fire) is reserved for the poor.

Irish Proverbs: The Wisdom of Silence

Silence is the fence around the haggard where wisdom is stacked.

Melodious is the closed mouth.

Who keeps his tongue keeps his friends.

Irish Proverbs: Human Nature

You never miss the water till the well runs dry.

Everyone feels his own wound first.

The pig in the sty doesn't know the pig going along the road.

Pity him who makes an opinion a certainty.

No two people ever lit a fire without disagreeing.

Seeing is believing, but feeling is the God's own truth.

It is the quiet pig that eats the meal.

A glowing gríosach (ember) is easily rekindled.

The person bringing good news knocks boldly on the door.

The Irish

A family of Irish birth will argue and fight, but let a shout come from without,and see them all unite.

An Irishman has an abiding sense of tragedy which sustains him through temporary periods of joy.

The Irish are a fair people; they never speak well of one another. — Samuel Johnson 1709-1784

The Irish forgive their great men when they are safely buried.

There are only three kinds of Irish men who can't understand women— young men, old men, and men of middle age.

☘ In the Irish
Is maith an t-anlann an t-ocras.
Hunger is a tasty sauce.

Ní hé lá na báistí lá na bpáistí
 A rainy day isn't a day for the children

Is deas an rud an beagán ach é a
dhéanamh go maith.
Little is best if well done.

Aithníonn ciaróg ciaróg eile
A beetle recognises another beetle

An té a chaillfeas a chlú, caillfidh
sé a náire.
 He who loses his reputation, loses
his shame.

Gura slán an scéalaí
May the bearer of the news be
safe.

Dá mbeifeá chomh láidir le crann
darach, gheobhadh an bás an
ceann is fearr ort.
 If you are as strong as an oak tree,
death will still vanquish you.

Is trom an t-ualach an leisce.
Laziness is a heavy burden.

Is maith an scáthán súil charad

A (true) friend's eye is a good
mirror

Bíonn dhá insint ar scéal agus dhá
leagan déag ar amhrán
There are two versions of/two
sides to every story & (at least)
twelve versions of every song.

Ní dhíolann dearmad fiacha.
 A debt is still unpaid, even if
forgotten.

Is leor don dreoilín a nead.
A wren only has need for its nest.

Ní cleas é go ndéantar trí huaire é.
It isn't a trick until it is done three
times.

Coimhéad fearg fhear na foighde.
Beware of the anger of a patient
man.

Maireann croí éadrom i bhfad.
A light heart lives longest.

Is iad na muca ciúine a itheann an
mhin.
 It is the quiet pigs that eat the
meal.

Is minic a bhris béal duine a
shrón.
Many a time a man's mouth broke
his nose.

Ní sheasann sac folamh.
An empty sack won't stand

Nár laga Dia do lámh May
 God not weaken your hand.

Teas gaoithe aduaidh nó fuacht
gaoithe aneas, sin báisteach.
The north wind's heat or the cold
of the south wind, means rain.

An té nach mbíonn láidir ní folláir
dó bheith glic
He who is not strong must needs
be cunning!

Is minic a rinne bromach gioblach
capall cumasach
An awkward colt often becomes a
beautiful horse .

Ni heolas go haontios
There is no knowledge without
unity

Ní hé lá na gaoithe lá na scoilbe.
A windy day is no day for
thatching.

Is leor nod don eolach.
A hint is sufficient for the wise.

An té a phósfas an t-airgead,
pósfaidh sé óinseach.
He who marries money, marries a
fool.

Is neamhbhuan cogadh na gcarad;
má bhíonn sé crua, ní bhíonn sé
fada.
A row between friends is short
lasting;, even if bitter it is never
long.

Is ón cheann a thagann an cheird.
The craft comes from the head.

Chomh sean leis an cheo agus níos
sine faoi dhó.
As old as the mist and older by
two.

Caill do chlú agus faigh ar ais é,
agus ní hé an rud céanna é.
Lose your reputation to regain it,
but it is never the same.

Dochtúir na sláinte an codladh.
Health's doctor is sleep.

Ná glac pioc comhairle gan
comhairle ban.
Never take advice without a
woman's guidance.

Maireann croi eadrom i bhfad."
A merry heart lives long.

"Nil aon tintean mar do thintean
fein."

There's no fireside like your own fireside.

"Coimhéad fearg fhear na foighde"
Beware of the anger of a patient man.

"Meallan muilte dé go mall ach meallan siad go mion."
God's mill may grind slowly, but it grinds finely.

"Dafheabhas e an t-ol is e an tart a dheireadh."
Good as drink is, it ends in thirst.

"Ní bhíonn airgead amadáin i bhfad ina phóca"

A fool's money is not long in his pocket.

"Níor bhris focal maith fiacail riamh"
A good word never broke a tooth.

"Is maith an t-anlann an t-ocras."
Hunger is the best sauce.

"Is minic a bhris beal duine a shron."
It's often a person's mouth breaks his nose.

"Is beo duine gan a chairde ach ni beo duine gan a phiopa."
One may live without one's friends, but not without one's pipe.

Irish Proverbs: Life's Ups & Downs and everything else.

There's nothing so bad that it couldn't be worse.

Life is a strange lad.

If God sends you down a stony path, may he give you strong shoes.

It's an ill wind that blows nobody good.

However long the day, night must fall.

You must take the little potato
with the big potato.

God prefers prayers to tears.

Questioning is the door of
knowledge.

The river is no wider from this side
than the other.

Seldom is the last of anything
better than the first.

God is good but don't dance in a
currach. (Boat)

A man without dinner— two for
supper.

One must pay health its tithe.

Earth has no sorrows that heaven
cannot heal.

You may as well give cherries to a pig as advice to a fool.

A nod is as good as a wink to a blind horse.

It's difficult to choose between two blind goats.

Even a tin knocker will shine on a dirty door.

It's no use carrying an umbrella if your shoes are leaking.

It's no use boiling your cabbage twice.

Never sell a hen on a wet day.

What I am afraid to hear I'd better say first myself.

If you move old furniture it may fall to bits.

Never dread the winter till the snow is on the blanket.

The man who pays the piper calls the tune.

Time and patience would bring a snail to America.

A good retreat is better than a bad stand.

The man with a cow doesn't need a scythe.

There's no point in keeping a dog if you are going to do your own barking.

Only a fool burns his coal without warming himself.

An oak is often split by a wedge from its own branch.

Every man's mind is his kingdom.

There are two things that cannot be cured: death and the want of sense.

Stupidity is sending the goose on a mission to the fox's den.

The fear of God is the beginning of wisdom.

Every finger has not the same length, nor every son the same disposition.

Every branch blossoms according to the root from which it sprung.

The friend that can be bought is not worth buying.

Blow not on dead embers.

They are scarce of news that speak ill of their mother.

Dead men tell no tales but there's many a thing learned in the wake-house.

Many a day shall we rest in the clay.

He who can follow his own will is a king.

If you dig a grave for others you may fall into it yourself.

Better fifty enemies outside the house than one within.

If you don't want flour on your clothes, stay out of the mill.

Drink is the curse of the land. It makes you fight with your neighbour. It makes you shoot at your landlord-- and it makes you miss him.

If you want to know what God thinks of money, just look at who He gives it to!

There never was the worse use made of a man than to hang him.

No man ever wore a scarf as warm as his daughter's arm around his neck.

You can accomplish more with a kind word and a shillelagh than you can with just a kind word.

In every land, hardness is in the north of it, softness in the south, industry in the east, and fire and inspiration in the west.

A drink precedes a story.

A friend's eye is a good mirror.

A hen is heavy when carried far.

A hound's food is in its legs.

A lock is better than suspicion.

A silent mouth is melodious.

A trade not properly learned is an enemy.

Age is honorable and youth is noble.

As the big hound is, so will the pup be.

Be neither intimate nor distant with the clergy.

Both your friend and your enemy think you will never die.

Even a small thorn causes festering.

Good as drink is, it ends in thirst.

He who comes with a story to you brings two away from you.

He who gets a name for early rising can stay in bed until midday.

If you do not sow in the spring you will not reap in the autumn.

If you want to be criticized, marry.

Instinct is stronger than upbringing.

It is a bad hen that does not scratch herself.

It is a long road that has no turning.

It is better to exist unknown to the law.

It is not a secret if it is known by three people.

It is sweet to drink but bitter to pay for.

It is the good horse that draws its own cart.

It is the quiet pigs that eat the meal.

It takes time to build castles. Rome wan not built in a day.

It's not a matter of upper and lower class but of being up a while and down a while.

Lack of resource has hanged many a person.

Listen to the sound of the river and you will get a trout.

May you have a bright future - as the chimney sweep said to his son.

Mere words do not feed the friars.

Nature breaks through the eyes of the cat.

Necessity is the mother of invention.

Necessity knows no law.

Need teaches a plan.

Patience is poultice for all wounds.

Youth does not mind where it sets its foot.

You've got to do your own growing, no matter how tall your grandfather was.

People live in each other's shelter.

Put silk on a goat, and it's still a goat.

Quiet people are well able to look after themselves.

The day will come when the cow will have use for her tail.

The hole is more honorable than the patch.

The light heart lives long.

The man with the boots does not mind where he places his foot.

The mills of God grind slowly but they grind finely.

The raggy colt often made a powerful horse.

The smallest thing outlives the human being.

The wearer best knows where the shoe pinches.

The well fed does not understand the lean.

The work praises the man.

The world would not make a racehorse of a donkey.

There is hope from the sea, but none from the grave.

There is no fireside like your own fireside.

There is no luck except where there is discipline.

There is no need like the lack of a friend.

There is no strength without unity.

Thirst is the end of drinking and sorrow is the end of drunkenness.

Three diseases without shame: Love, itch and thirst.

Time is a great story teller.

Two shorten the road.

Two thirds of the work is the semblance.

Walk straight, my son - as the old crab said to the young crab.

When a twig grows hard it is difficult to twist it. Every beginning is weak.

When fire is applied to a stone it cracks.

When the apple is ripe it will fall.

When the drop (drink) is inside, the sense is outside.

When the liquor was gone the fun was gone.

Wine divulges truth.

You cannot make a silk purse out of a sow's ear.

You must live with a person to know a person. If you want to know me come and live with me.

Youth sheds many a skin.

The steed (horse) does not retain its speed forever.

Never bolt the door with a boiled carrot.

Man is incomplete until he marries. After that, he is finished.

Three things come without asking: fear, jealousy, and love.

Idleness is a fool's desire.

Good luck beats early rising.

If a cat had a dowry, she would often be kissed.

To the raven her own chick is white.

Everyone praises his native land.

A diplomat must always think twice before he says nothing.

A heavy purse makes for a light heart.

Those who get the name of rising early may lie all day.

A lie travels further than the truth.

Marriages are all happy. It's having breakfast together that causes all the trouble.

A man loves his sweetheart the most, his wife the best, but his mother the longest.

A scholars ink lasts longer than a martyrs blood.

If you want an audience start a fight.

Don't break your shin on a stool that is not in your way.

If you dig a grave for others, you might fall into it yourself.

What will come from the briar but the berry.

A poem ought to be well made at first, for there is many a one to spoil it afterwards.

The Irish forgive their great men when they are safely buried.

A change of work is as good as a rest.

A good retreat is better than a bad stand.

Drink is the curse of the land. It makes you fight with your neighbor. It makes you shoot at your landlord and it makes you miss him.

A spender gets the property of the hoarder.

Never tell secrets to your relatives' children.

Put a beggar on a horse and he'll ride it to hell.

Cheerfulness is a sign of wisdom.

It's not a delay to stop and sharpen the scythe.

Only the rich can afford compassion.

There's many a ship lost within sight of the harbor.

The dog that's always on the go is better than one that's always curled up.

Listen to the sound of the river and you will get a trout.

It is a long road that has no turning.

An ounce of breeding is worth a pound of feeding.

Horse racing expression meaning that thoroughbreds are born and not made.

The day will come when the cow will have use for her tail.

May you live as long as you want, and never want as long as you live.

Necessity knows no law.

As the Irish say it

(Of a useless fellow) He's fit to mind mice at a crossroads.

(To someone who committed some small fault) 'Tis only a stepmother would blame you.'

(Of a tall, large woman) That's a fine doorful of a woman.

(Of a gossip) She has a tongue that would clip a hedge.

(Of a poor, thin creature) The breath is only just in and out of him, and the grass doesn't know of him walking over it.

(Of an ill-mannered person) What would you expect out of a pig but a grunt?

(On trying to change a stubborn person's mind) You might as well be whistling jigs to a milestone.

(Of bad music) Aw, that's the tune the old cow died of.

(Of one who overstays their welcome) If that man went to a wedding, he'd stay for the christening.

(Of a talkative person) That man would talk the teeth out of a saw.

(Of a person who paid too much for a cow) He bought every hair in her tail.

(Of a clever thief) He'd steal the sugar out of your punch.

(In praise of strong whiskey) I felt it like a torchlight procession going down my throat.

(Said of a woman who had made a bad marriage) She burnt her coal and did not warm herself.

(Of a bad aim) He wouldn't hit a hole in a ladder.

(Of an impish child) That one suffers from a double dose of original sin.

(Of an unfortunate one) He is always in the field when luck is on the road.

(Of very wet weather) It's a fine day for young ducks.

(Of someone who always plans carefully) If he's not fishing he's mending his nets.

Youth

Praise the young and they will flourish.

Praise youth and it will prosper.

You've got to do your own growing, no matter how tall your grandfather was.

❧ Christmas Proverbs

"Téann an saol thart mar a bheadh eiteoga air, agus cuireann gach aon
Nollaig bliain eile ar do ghualainn." (**Life goes as quickly as if it had wings, and each Christmas places another year on your shoulders**.)

"Bia is deoch i gcomhair na Nollag; éadach nua i gcomhair na Cásca." (**Eat and drink on Christmas – for Easter new clothing.**)

"Putóga dubha na bliana, ó Nollaig go Lá Fhéile Bríde." (**From Christmas day until St.**

Bridgit's feast is the darkest part of the year.)

"Nollaig ghlas, reilig mhéith. **(A green Christmas brings a full graveyard.)**

Is úr iad broibh go Nollaig."
(Grass stalks stay fresh until Christmas)

"Tuor maith don athbhliain na píobairí teallaigh a chloisteáil Lá Nollag." **(Hearing crickets on Christmas is a good omen for the new year.)**

"Aifreann na Gine, Aifreann agus fiche." **(One midnight Mass is worth twenty-one regular Masses)**

Proverbs

A diplomat must always think twice before he says nothing.

A dog owns nothing, yet is seldom dissatisfied.

A hair on the head is worth two on the brush.

A kind word never broke anyone's mouth.

A lie travels farther than the truth.

A light heart lives long.

A silent mouth is sweet to hear.

A turkey never voted for an early Christmas.

Better be quarrelling than lonesome.

Bricks and mortar make a house, but the laughter of children makes a home.

Don't break your shin on a stool that is not in your way.

Even the longest day has its end.

Give away all you like, but keep your bills and your temper.

Good luck beats early rising.

If you dig a grave for others, you might fall into it yourself.

If you get a reputation as an early riser, you can sleep till noon.

It's no use carrying an umbrella if your shoes are leaking.

The believer is happy, the doubter is wise.

Irish Toasts

May your glass be ever full.

May the roof over your head be always strong.

And may you be in heaven half an hour before the devil knows you're dead.

Health and life to you; The mate of your choice to you; Land without rent to you, and death in Eirinn.